Contents

MALLARMÉ'S
L'APRÈS-MIDI D'UN FAUNE

AN EXEGETICAL AND
CRITICAL STUDY

A. R. CHISHOLM

Professor Emeritus of French
University of Melbourne

MELBOURNE UNIVERSITY PRESS
on behalf of
THE AUSTRALIAN HUMANITIES RESEARCH COUNCIL

First published 1958
Printed in Australia by Melbourne University Press
Carlton, N.3, Victoria

Registered in Australia for transmission
by post as a book

London and New York: Cambridge University Press

Text

Le Faune

Ces nymphes, je les veux perpétuer.
                              Si clair,
Leur incarnat léger, qu'il voltige dans l'air
Assoupi de sommeils touffus.
                              Aimai-je un rêve?
Mon doute, amas de nuit ancienne, s'achève
En maint rameau subtil, qui, demeuré les vrais   5
Bois mêmes, prouve, hélas! que bien seul je m'offrais
Pour triomphe la faute idéale de roses.
Réfléchissons . . .

                    ou si les femmes dont tu gloses
Figurent un souhait de tes sens fabuleux!
Faune, l'illusion s'échappe des yeux bleus   10
Et froids, comme une source en pleurs, de la plus chaste :
Mais, l'autre, tout soupirs, dis-tu qu'elle contraste
Comme brise du jour chaude dans ta toison?
Que non! par l'immobile et lasse pâmoison
Suffoquant de chaleurs le matin frais s'il lutte,   15
Ne murmure point d'eau que ne verse ma flûte
Au bosquet arrosé d'accords; et le seul vent
Hors des deux tuyaux prompt à s'exhaler avant
Qu'il disperse le son dans une pluie aride,
C'est, à l'horizon pas remué d'une ride,   20
Le visible et serein souffle artificiel
De l'inspiration, qui regagne le ciel.

O bords siciliens d'un calme marécage
Qu'à l'envi de soleils ma vanité saccage,
Tacite sous les fleurs d'étincelles, CONTEZ   25
'Que je coupais ici les creux roseaux domptés
'Par le talent; quand, sur l'or glauque de lointaines

5

'Verdures dédiant leur vigne à des fontaines,
'Ondoie une blancheur animale au repos:
'Et qu'au prélude lent où naissent les pipeaux   30
'Ce vol de cygnes, non! de naïades se sauve
'Ou plonge . . .'

        Inerte, tout brûle dans l'heure fauve
Sans marquer par quel art ensemble détala
Trop d'hymen souhaité de qui cherche le *la*:
Alors m'éveillerai-je à la ferveur première,   35
Lys! et l'un de vous tous pour l'ingénuité.

Autre que ce doux rien par leur lèvre ébruité,
Le baiser, qui tout bas des perfides assure,
Mon sein, vierge de preuve, atteste une morsure   40
Mystérieuse, due à quelque auguste dent;
Mais, bast! arcane tel élut pour confident
Le jonc vaste et jumeau dont sous l'azur on joue:
Qui, détournant à soi le trouble de la joue,
Rêve, dans un solo long, que nous amusions   45
La beauté d'alentour par des confusions
Fausses entre elle-même et notre chant crédule;
Et de faire aussi haut que l'amour se module
Evanouir du songe ordinaire de dos
Ou de flanc pur suivis avec mes regards clos,   50
Une sonore, vaine et monotone ligne.

Tâche donc, instrument des fuites, ô maligne
Syrinx, de refleurir aux lacs où tu m'attends!
Moi, de ma rumeur fier, je vais parler longtemps
Des déesses; et par d'idolâtres peintures,   55
A leur ombre enlever encore des ceintures:
Ainsi, quand des raisins j'ai sucé la clarté,
Pour bannir un regret par ma feinte écarté,
Rieur, j'élève au ciel d'été la grappe vide
Et, soufflant dans ses peaux lumineuses, avide   60
D'ivresse, jusqu'au soir je regarde au travers.

O nymphes, regonflons des SOUVENIRS divers.
'Mon œil, trouant les joncs, dardait chaque encolure
'Immortelle, qui noie en l'onde sa brûlure
'Avec un cri de rage au ciel de la forêt;   65
'Et le splendide bain de cheveux disparaît

'Dans les clartés et les frissons, ô pierreries!
'J'accours; quand, à mes pieds, s'entrejoignent (meurtries
'De la langueur goûtée à ce mal d'être deux)
'Des dormeuses parmi leurs seuls bras hasardeux;   70
'Je les ravis, sans les désenlacer, et vole
'A ce massif, haï par l'ombrage frivole,
'De roses tarissant tout parfum au soleil,
'Où notre ébat au jour consumé soit pareil.'
Je t'adore, courroux des vierges, ô délice   75
Farouche du sacré fardeau nu qui se glisse
Pour fuir ma lèvre en feu buvant, comme un éclair
Tressaille! la frayeur secrète de la chair:
Des pieds de l'inhumaine au cœur de la timide
Que délaisse à la fois une innocence, humide   80
De larmes folles ou de moins tristes vapeurs.
'Mon crime, c'est d'avoir, gai de vaincre ces peurs
'Traîtresses, divisé la touffe échevelée
'De baisers que les dieux gardaient si bien mêlée:
'Car, à peine j'allais cacher un rire ardent   85
'Sous les replis heureux d'une seule (gardant
'Par un doigt simple, afin que sa candeur de plume
'Se teignît à l'émoi de sa sœur qui s'allume,
'La petite, naïve et ne rougissant pas:)
'Que de mes bras, défaits par de vagues trépas,   90
'Cette proie, à jamais ingrate se délivre
'Sans pitié du sanglot dont j'étais encore ivre.'

Tant pis! vers le bonheur d'autres m'entraîneront
Par leur tresse nouée aux cornes de mon front:
Tu sais, ma passion, que, pourpre et déjà mûre,   95
Chaque grenade éclate et d'abeilles murmure;
Et notre sang, épris de qui le va saisir,
Coule pour tout l'essaim éternel du désir.
A l'heure où ce bois d'or et de cendres se teinte
Une fête s'exalte en la feuillée éteinte: 100
Etna! c'est parmi toi visité de Vénus
Sur ta lave posant ses talons ingénus,
Quand tonne un somme triste ou s'épuise la flamme.
Je tiens la reine!
            O sûr châtiment . . .
                        Non, mais l'âme

De paroles vacante et ce corps alourdi   105
Tard succombent au fier silence de midi :
Sans plus il faut dormir en l'oubli du blasphème,
Sur le sable altéré gisant et comme j'aime
Ouvrir ma bouche à l'astre efficace des vins !

Couple, adieu; je vais voir ~~voir~~ l'ombre que tu devins.

I

Time and Topography

L'Après-Midi d'un Faune is, next to the *Coup de Dés*, the poem in which Mallarmé has gone furthest in 'musicalising' poetry. It is more beautiful than the *Coup de Dés*, because the framework of the musical structure is more subtle than in the lengthier piece, and there is less recourse to the device of typographical variations, which are rather foreign to poetry.

In *l'Après-Midi* the only special typography takes the form of italics, quite justified here, because they indicate a long, but interrupted, quotation within the monologue; a careful notation made by the Faun's lucid mind, when his drowsy self occasionally throws off its somnolence and records the events of the morning. To me, these italicised passages almost suggest a parchment, on which a hand writes with clear calligraphy but lets its pen drop as sleepiness or doubt slackens its muscles.

In this mixture of lucid and somnolent thought time-notations are most important; and thanks to the musicality of the whole, these notations are rather difficult to grasp. As in music, everything here is fluid; past and present fade into each other; so that occasionally, when the Faun seems to be speaking of the present, he is actually referring to the past; that is to say that when he appears to be alluding to the afternoon he is thinking of the events of the morning.

Thus in lines 14-22 it might easily be supposed that he is referring to the *present* sound of his flute ('ne *murmure* point d'eau que ne *verse* ma flûte'. 'Le seul vent . . . *c'est* . . . le visible et serein souffle artificiel'). But closer scrutiny of the text shows that this is impossible, for within this passage, in line 15, he refers explicitly to 'le matin frais', whereas the monologue belongs to the early afternoon (early, seeing that in line 106 the Faun mentions the 'fier silence de midi', which must still be hanging over him like a soporific haze). The syrinx is now really an *absence* — which is natural enough in a poem by Mallarmé.

Again, he uses the present tense, 'rêve', in reference to his flute (line 45). But the verb that really fixes the time is a preterite, 'élut' (line 42). Once more, he is intent upon what happened in the morning.

Having determined these time-notations, we shall find it easier to elucidate the otherwise puzzling command in lines 52-53:

Tâche donc, instrument des fuites, ô maligne
Syrinx, de refleurir aux lacs où tu m'attends.

The Faun had cut and used his pipes in the morning, and then left them beside the 'lakes' where he saw, or thought he saw, the nymphs. We have to conclude, therefore, that in addressing his syrinx in this cryptic fashion he is really dismissing it, bidding it wait beside the water where he had left it ('où tu m'attends'), like a reed flowering among the lilies. *Why* he dismisses it is a question that will be examined later.

Another feature in these time-notations needs to be noticed: the passages in italics all refer to the past. It is a past (the morning) reconstructed pictorially; for memory falls back readily on pictures. This plastic element is greatly strengthened in the second of the italicised passages, where we find a superb picture of the nymphs, startled and plunging into the water; superb, but superbly condensed into two lines, 66-67, which will be further discussed in our Interpretation.

Topography is no less important than time-notations for an appreciation of the poem. It may seem rather a crude term to apply to so airy a structure; but it is here intended to mean no more than the coherence of the picture that was in Mallarmé's mind as he wrote.

For the solution of this and other problems of interpretation considerable help is afforded by the existence of two earlier versions of *l'Après-Midi*. These are the *Monologue d'un Faune*, which Mallarmé began, apparently in 1865, with an eye to actual performance of the piece at the Comédie Française; and the *Improvisation d'un Faune*, completed ten years later for the third series of *Le Parnasse Contemporain*, but rejected (!) by the editorial committee. The final version was first published in a plaquette, with 'decorations' by Manet, early in 1876 (Mallarmé speaks of the publisher as 'M. Alphonse Derenne, le *publisher* de *la République des Lettres*'). This became the 'definitive' version in the edition published by the *Revue Indépendante* in 1887. The two earlier versions are given, with many useful notes, in the invaluable Pléiade edition of Mallarmé's *œuvres Complètes,* by Henri Mondor and G. Jean-Aubry.

The landscape of the poem, as first conceived by Mallarmé, was not vast; and it is reasonable to suppose that this first conception remained more or less constant during the long years that passed between the earliest and the definitive version. It was in Sicily, in the neighbourhood of Mount Etna (line 101).

The 'vrais bois mêmes' (lines 5-6) near which the Faun awakens are apparently identical with the 'massif' (line 72) to which he thought he had carried the nymphs. For in the *Improvisation* the lines corresponding to lines 5-6 of the definitive version are as follows:

> En de nouveaux rameaux; qui, demeurés ces vrais
> Massifs noirs, font qu'hélas! . . .

Further, these woods ('bosquet' in line 17, 'massif' in line 72) must have been conceived by the poet as being fairly close to both the marsh (line 23) where he cut the reeds for his flute, and the 'fontaines' (line 28) or 'lacs' (line 53) where he thought he saw the nymphs. That the trees were close to the lakes is proved by sheer logic: the Faun carried the nymphs thither from the lakeside; and mythology does not specifically assure us that nymphs were featherweights.

The marsh, in turn, must have been fairly close to the lakes, for the Faun saw the nymphs plunge into the water as he watched them through the reeds (line 63), and could distinguish the rippling and splashing of the water (lines 66-67).

It is particularly important that the trees should be close to the marsh; for this detail affects the interpretation of the beautiful passage in lines 14-22. As I see it, the music poured out on to these woods came from the edge of the marsh where the Faun tuned his pipes ('cherche le *la*', line 34).

We can now sketch out the landscape, and sum up the events remembered or imagined by the Faun, as follows. He cut the reeds, and made his syrinx, at the edge of the marsh. Then, as he peered through the reeds, he saw some white forms resting

beside waters overhung by '*de lointaines verdures*'. '*Lointaines*'
is surely not 'far away', but merely 'at some distance', for reasons
already mentioned.

The sound of his pipes, as he tuned them, startled the nymphs,
all of whom, except two, fled away or plunged into the water.
He ran to the lakeside and there found two sleeping nymphs,
clasped in each other's arms; carried them to the neighbouring
woods, *dropping his pipes beside the water.*

After the sensual episode described in lines 71-92 the picture
fades; so that the Faun remembers neither when he fell asleep,
nor whether he had seen the nymphs in a dream. All this
vagueness has a special aesthetic purpose, as we shall see when
discussing the Intention of the poem. But on this shadowy background the 'topographical' details still have their importance.
Without them, any coherent interpretation of *l'Après-Midi d'un
Faune* is impossible.

II

Themes

Since, in *l'Après-Midi d'un Faune*, Mallarmé is trying to make poetry do what music alone can normally do, we expect to find several themes running through the poem; interwoven, fading into each other, emerging, disappearing, reappearing, in the ordinary musical manner. There are, apparently, four such themes.

The first, which we shall call, for convenience, the Sensuality theme, appears in the opening lines and often re-emerges from the general structure. The Faun, frustrated by his own drowsiness in the heat of the early afternoon, is trying to recapture an erotic episode. His whole being is a texture of vibrant sensuality; and though the nymphs have vanished, his hot desire sees in the air about him the memory of their inviting flesh.

The second theme seeks an explanation of the nymphs and of their disappearance. Perhaps they were only a dream ('Aimai-je un rêve?'). We shall call this the Dream theme. It is at first dismissed by logic (lines 4-7); then goes on immediately, merging into the hypothesis of a day-dream, a hot vision engendered by the Faun's own ardent senses (lines 8-9). This possibility is again dismissed by logic, and occurs no more until it is vaguely suggested, perhaps, in the closing lines. Yet, in a subtle way, it haunts the whole poem; it is unheard but ever-present, latent in all the other themes, whispering just below the level of perceptibility.

The logic that dismissed this dream and day-dream hypothesis passes into, or propounds, a new theme, a very beautiful one, which we can call the Art theme. It is introduced in lines 14-22, where the Faun realises that music can create atmosphere, suggest a murmuring stream, a summer breeze. Later, this theme shows how art can transform reality. It becomes an important part of the poet's Intention, which will be discussed later under that heading.

Finally, there is the Memory theme, seeking to reconstruct episodes that took place or could have taken place. To make sure of their substantial quality, the Faun associates these memories with the actual marsh where he had cut his pipes (line 23); then with the nymphs, envisaged as beings of flesh and blood (line 62).

The Memory theme is printed in italics, which seems to indicate that Mallarmé wanted it to stand out from the rest. The possible reason for this will be discussed later, when we are considering the poet's Intention.

The arrangement and interweaving of the four themes is as follows.

As we have seen, the Sensuality theme is enunciated in the opening lines. Naturally enough, it passes into the Dream theme in line 3; for the Faun, despite his sensual excitement, is still half asleep. The Dream, soon scouted by logic, is succeeded in line 8 by a variation, the Day-Dream. Immediately (line 10) logic disposes of it, preparing the way for the Art theme, which begins with line 14 and runs on to the end of the stanza. When it ends (line 22), there is a pause, indicated by the spacing.

Then the Memory theme, preceded by a short introductory passage, emerges for the first time (lines 26-31 and the first two syllables of line 32). It is, here as elsewhere, in italics.

The Sensuality theme asserts itself more lengthily than before in lines 32-37. Then the Art theme emerges in full strength, occupying a whole stanza (lines 38-51), with echoes of the Sensuality theme in lines 38, 39, 49 and 50 — a characteristically musical structure.

It is time now for the Sensuality theme to be more fully enunciated, and it in turn occupies a whole stanza (lines 52-61); though the way for the recurrent Memory theme, essentially pictorial, is prepared by the splendid plastic images at the end of the stanza.

With line 63 the Memory theme emerges boldly, after an introductory line, and runs right on to line 74. It is succeeded by a recurrence of the Sensuality theme, which runs from line 75 to line 81 and is then replaced by a new emergence of the Memory theme. Notice that these two great themes, Memory and Sensuality, are bound together in one long stanza (lines 62-92) as Mallarmé prepares for his finale.

This finale, beginning with line 93, is chiefly devoted to the Sensuality theme. But there are suggestions (without italics) of the plastic Memory theme in the imagery of lines 94-96, with a subdued and dimmed, almost fluid, plastic image in line 99. And at last the Sensuality theme, which had been softened into vagueness by the Faun's somnolence at the beginning of the poem, passes over once more into a sleepy yearning, a half-dream that suggests, but does not develop, the earlier Dream theme.

III

Interpretation

As Mallarmé once remarked, in an often quoted conversation with Degas, poetry is written with words. And words tell a story of some kind. Let us then, without forcing its subtle musicality into too rigid a mould of elucidation, examine the 'argument' of the poem.

The scene is in Sicily, in the early part of a hot afternoon. The Faun, who has been sleeping in the warm air and is still only half awake, is trying to recall how he caught the two nymphs before he fell asleep; endeavouring to fix ('perpétuer') the details of their appearance.

Nothing remains of them except a somnolent memory; yet his impressions are still so lively that the glow of their colouring seems to be fluttering in the slumbrous air. It is interesting to remark that this notation had been more precise and sensual in the *Monologue d'un Faun,* where we find:

> .... le clair
> Rubis des seins levés embrase encore l'air.

Mallarmé has greatly improved this in the definitive version, where there is less precision, a vagueness more appropriate to the moment of the Faun's awakening. The air is still heavy with dreams; and the colour in the air, the Faun tells himself, may represent the last shreds of a dream. Incidentally, it looks as if Mallarmé, influenced perhaps by the Latin *somnium-somnia,* cognate with *somnus,* uses the rare plural, 'sommeils', in the sense of 'dreams'.

Dream or reality? The heaviness of sleep ('amas de nuit ancienne') has left the Faun uncertain. But his uncertainty seems to be dispelled 'Mon doute . . . s'achève') as he grows more lucid and alert. For each branch, that had appeared so tenuous and dream-like ('subtil') as he looked at it on awakening, through drowsy, half-closed eyes, is now being gradually transformed into a part of 'les vrais bois mêmes'. Therefore, he concludes, he had actually been in this thicket, not dreamed that he had been there.

The lines in the *Improvisation d'un Faune* that correspond to lines 5-7 in our text help us to elucidate this difficult passage. They are as follows:

> En de nouveaux rameaux; qui, demeurés ces vrais
> Massifs noirs, font qu'hélas! tout à l'heure j'ouvrais
> Les yeux à la pudeur ordinaire de roses.

Thus what he had seen was no more than roses; ordinary, blushing roses; and it was their colour that had suggested, to his sleepy and overheated imagination, the colouring of the nymphs. The yielding of the nymphs – or of one of them – had been only a 'faute idéale de roses'; a mere transformation of blushing roses into a sensual surrender (*faute* in the sense of a moral lapse is amply attested by Littré).

Immediately the Faun proposes (lines 8-9) a new hypothesis. Perhaps this apparition, at first mistaken for a dream, had been an hallucination engendered by his ardent desire, his 'sens fabuleux'. This use of *fabuleux,* imaginative, is justified by the Latin *fabulosus,* which can mean 'rich in fables' as well as 'fabulous'.

However, he has to dismiss this new hypothesis. How could the *hot* senses of a faun conceive by sheer imagination the *cold* blue eyes that characterised one of the two nymphs? (lines 10-11). True, the other nymph, 'tout soupirs' and quite different ('elle contraste') from her companion, might well have been created by his ardent imagination. A warm breeze blowing through his fleece might have sufficed to suggest her presence.

But there was no breeze: he remembers that detail. The morning had been filled with motionless, wearying, soporific heat ('pâmoison'), which choked the early freshness if it tried to assert itself ('s'il lutte'). There was no murmuring water, that might have suggested a lake; no liquid sound at all except that of his pipes, which drenched the neighbouring thicket with melody. And the only wind was that which he blew into his flute, and which moved up, transformed by art ('artificiel') into sweet sounds, towards the sky, towards the god who had inspired his song. (This god is evoked again later, in line 41, by the phrase 'auguste dent').

The beautiful passage (lines 14-22) in which these thoughts about music and its creative power are expressed, is itself a lovely melody. Notice the liquid quality (corresponding to the sense and the intention) of the numerous *l* sounds; and the *m* sounds in the murmuring lines with which the passage begins. Notice also the liquid musicality of the images: the 'immobile et lasse pâmoison' of the warm air; the 'bosquet arrosé d'accords'; the breath which the musician transforms into an elusive visible entity.

Having thus disposed of the hypothesis of an hallucination created by his hot senses, the Faun now sets out to recall in detail what he had seen in the morning, beginning with the marsh where he had cut reeds for his syrinx; for the marsh and the reeds were realities beyond all doubt. He had ransacked this marsh as eagerly as the hot sun did day after day, searching for reeds that would satisfy his musical vanity; the marsh that lay silent under the clustering coruscations of the sunlight ('fleurs d'étincelles'). And this is what he succeeds in reconstructing:

He was cutting the reeds that were to be put at the service of his art ('talent'), when, against a background of greenery which, some distance away, hung down over the water, he saw a shimmering whiteness that appeared to be living forms at rest. But when he blew his first tentative notes, the sound startled these creatures (Swans? No, naiads surely! says the Faun); some scampered off, while others plunged into the lake.

He cannot pursue this clear line of thought, for he is again feeling the drowsy influence of the afternoon. In the heat and inertia of this 'heure fauve' he cannot recall how ('par quel art', line 33) all those nymphs, over-hotly desired ('trop d'hymen souhaité'), on whom his eyes were eagerly fixed as he tuned his pipes, scampered away simultaneously. ('Heure fauve' is a marvellously compact phrase. The heat is fierce, like *un fauve;* the air is tawny, yellow with sunshine).

Though there is no question-mark in the text, lines 35-37 are interrogative, as indicated in the *Improvisation,* which has:

> M'éveillerai-je donc de ma langueur première,
> Droit et seul, sous un flot d'ironique lumière,
> Lys; et parmi vous tous, beau d'ingénuité?

The questions seem to be these: 'Now that I am awake, shall I find only the blank, uneasy, hot and unfulfilled desire that I felt at first ('ferveur première'), before I saw those white forms? Shall I be only like the lilies at the water's edge, standing alone, waiting ingenuously for fulfilment of my burning desires, just as the ingenuous lilies have to be content with the un-differentiated ardour of the sunlight? Shall I find that nothing really happened?'

In the above interpretation, 'pour' has been taken in the sense of *à cause de* in the phrase 'pour l'ingénuité'; so that, with its context, the latter can be paraphrased as 'A cause de mon ingénuité, ô lys, serai-je un de vous tous?' This meaning of *pour* is given a prominent place by Littré, who quotes, among other things, La Fontaine's phrase: 'On abattit un pin pour son antiquité', *Fables*, XI. 9 *(Les Souris et le Chat-Huant)*.

This leads the Faun (lines 38-51) back to the Art theme. There is on his body no sign ('preuve') of any hot encounter; no sign other than the memory, or fancied memory, of a kiss; no sign other than a voice within him that seems to evoke the sound of a kiss and to assure him that the unfaithful nymphs had really existed.

True, there is on his breast another mark, invisible yet real: the mysterious sign left by the bite of a deity, the god of music. But that mysterious visitation ('arcane') did not choose the nymphs to express itself; it whispered its secrets in the only way possible to it, into the two reeds of the syrinx. And the syrinx sublimated the Faun's fiery yearnings into a simple melody. The ardent, restless mouth ('joue'), breathing into the pipes, transferred its ardent restlessness to them. A melodious dream beguiled (a normal meaning of *amuser*) the landscape, blending ('confusions') its *visible* beauty with the *audible*, imaginative ('crédule') beauty of music; so that (though the analogy was false) sight became sound, and sound became sight.

Thus the Faun's ordinary, sensual day-dream, through closed eyes, about white backs and white flanks, was transformed; and on the high level where passion becomes music ('l'amour se module'), a simple melody, devoid of material content, 'Une sonore, vaine et monotone ligne', faded away ('évanouir') into the air, up towards the god who had inspired it (cf. line 22).

That is an exquisite definition of music, which, with its

strange sublimations, goes beyond the individual data of the senses and expresses the pure Idea inherent in them. And by one of those miracles of which Mallarmé possessed the secret, this definition is itself a flawless piece of music.

In the passage just discussed, the Faun had risen above his ordinary self; the artist in him had outsoared the animal. And now, by a natural reaction, his libidinous animality reasserts itself. He dismisses music, bidding his syrinx wait for him by the lake, real or imaginary, where he had left it when he seized the two nymphs. This will leave him free to gloat over his fiercely sensual memories; to boast of his conquests; to imagine himself ('idolâtres' is based on *idole,* which is, etymologically, an image) tearing their girdle from other nymphs. And then, the artist in him asserting itself in another way, he compares these pleasures of recollection with the delight that he found by blowing into empty grape-skins and looking at the light as it shone through them.

This brings him back quite naturally to the Memory theme (line 62), the verb 'regonflons' constituting a link between the two passages ('As I breathed new life into the grapes, let us now breathe new life into this morning's memories').

In the opening lines of this recurrent Memory theme the plastic artist who had painted that splendid picture of the grapes again predominates; and the Faun gives us a vivid picture of what he saw, or thought he saw, beside the lake. As he peered through the reeds, his gaze was so eager that it projected ('dardait') the forms of the nymphs on to the screen of his eager anticipation. He watched each hot body plunge into the lake, with a 'cri de rage' that echoed the hammering of his own burning senses. And when those splendid forms, with outspread tresses, met the water, they were like shimmerings of light ('clartés'). They sent out widening ripples ('frissons'), and particles of water were thrown up, sparkling like precious stones.

The Faun hastened to the spot, and found two nymphs still asleep, clasped in each other's arms, in an unconscious ('hasardeux') embrace, as if even in their sleep each felt the wretchedness of being alone.

He seized them and carried them off to the thicket, which was steeped in sunlight, the wandering, fickle shade having left it (line 72). It was so hot that the perfume of the roses was consumed by the sun. His sensual instincts had brought him thither, so that his amorous delights might be as hot as the burning air.

This memory, real or fanciful, has now become so vivid that for a while the Faun abandons his reconstruction of it, to gloat over the experience as if it were now really being enacted – hence the return to present tenses in lines 75-81. What a delight it is, he cries exultantly, to watch this virginal anger, as the nymphs try to elude my burning kisses! My lips dart like lightning from one part of their trembling bodies to another, drinking in the fear that roves from the feet of the nymph with the cold blue eyes ('l'inhumaine'; cf. lines 10-11) to the breast of the other. The latter is timid but not cold, for her innocence is already forsaking her (line 80). She is wet with tears of shame and anger – or perhaps, thinks the lecherous Faun, her body is moist with passion ('moins tristes vapeurs').

Then he comes back to his less impatient reconstruction of the episode, back to the Memory theme. He recalls his great mistake, his crime against himself. That single word, 'crime', is an epitome of unbridled passion, which makes its own ethics and looks on every frustration as a sin.

His 'crime' had consisted of separating the two nymphs, whom the gods of hazard had bound together in their sleep. He had given all his ardent attention to one of them, holding the other with one hand so that she might, in her snowy innocence, feel the contagion of her companion's growing passion. This loosened his grasp, his arms already being weakened by sensual excitement ('vagues trépas'); and so the more passionate nymph slipped from his embrace, unpitying and ungrateful (the supreme egotism of his desire is again making its own ethics).

There follows a silence, indicated by the spacing, during which we have to imagine that the Faun, carried away by the vividness of these recollections, is invaded by a consuming, unreasoning, no longer analytic passion. He then returns to the Sensuality theme.

He will, he says, find other nymphs who will be more compliant. For this is the season of warm passions. The pomegranates are bursting, and bees are swarming around their luscious pulp. So also the eternal swarming of desires fills the

summer air, and the blood of all fauns is palpitating in tune
with this universal passion.

These lines bring out the consistent musicality of the poem;
for they are a loud, triumphant echo, in a major key, of the
Sensuality theme which had begun with a quieter quivering
of desire, an evanescent palpitation in the hot, drowsy air:

> . . . . . . Si clair,
> Leur incarnat léger, qu'il voltige dans l'air
> Assoupi de sommeils touffus.

The swarming palpitations are loud and passionate this time,
as one might expect in the finale; louder and more passionate,
even, than the passionate cry of the Muse in Musset's *Nuit de
Mai:*

> Poète, prends ton luth; le vin de la jeunesse
> Fermente cette nuit dans les veines de Dieu.

But in conformity with the original enunciation of the theme,
the 'sommeils touffus' will presently return.

In the wildness of his desire the Faun remembers that he is
near Etna, the dwelling-place of Vulcan; and that sometimes
at dusk, when the low sun is spreading an ashen-gold glow over
the woods, and when the volcano is emitting a sleepy rumble,
or its flame is dying down, there is an exhilaration in the barely
visible leaves. It is caused by the presence of Venus. (Notice how
beautifully the ash-gold glow of sunset mirrors the quiescent
fire of Etna) . . . His impudent thought is: 'I shall capture the
Goddess herself!'

But even in his growing somnolence (indicated by the spacing,
which suggests drowsy hesitation) he remembers the sure punish-
ment that would follow . . . His mind is now almost empty of
thought; both it and his body are succumbing at last ('tard')
to the hot silence that the noon had brought . . . He must forget
that blasphemous thought about Venus . . . and sleep once
more; lying on the hot, thirsty sand, and opening his mouth,
as he loves to do, to the sun that ripens grapes and makes wine
possible.

And then the poem closes with a line that possibly recalls,
briefly and dimly, the Dream motif. The Faun will pass once
more into the darkness of slumber, in which, perhaps, the dream

of the two nymphs had come to him. Maybe he will renew his dream and find them again; for they have passed also into the kingdom of darkness, the realm of sleep. This interpretation of the last line is suggested by the use of the verb 'voir': 'I am going to *see* the kingdom of darkness and the dream-forms that move in it'.

Postscript

To avoid interruption of the general 'argument', the following remarks have been reserved for a postscript. In an early passage (lines 4-7) the Faun thinks that he had, in the transition from sleep to consciousness, taken roses for rosy nymphs, because he had seen these roses through a haze of somnolence.

This is an accurate psychological notation, transmuted into art. Actually, when one is, in the sunlight, becoming drowsy or slowly awakening, the surroundings have a tenuous, nebulous character. A branch is, like Mallarmé's 'rameau subtil', almost unreal, only half-seen, blurred into unreality by the wakening or waning of the imagination.

Heredia describes this admirably in a sonnet, *La Sieste*, where he weaves the fading forms of the landscape into a web of light, wherein are caught the imaginings that are still sleepily conscious, but already of the same stuff as dreams:

> Alors mes doigts tremblants saisissent chaque fil,
> Et dans les mailles d'or de ce filet subtil,
> Chasseur harmonieux, j'emprisonne mes rêves.

By a curious coincidence, *La Sieste* belongs to the same year (1876) as the Derenne edition of the *Après-Midi d'un Faune*.

IV

Intention

It is rather like breaking a butterfly on the wheel to seek in a poem, and particularly in as airy and elusive a composition as *l'Après-Midi d'un Faune,* the sort of background that a philosophical treatise usually has. It would, therefore, be rather temerarious to credit Mallarmé with a knowledge of German romantic philosophy in general and, in particular, a close acquaintance with the work of Schopenhauer.

Although his wife was a native speaker of German, it is practically certain that any such knowledge was in his case indirect, gleaned from articles in magazines and from journalistic vulgarisations.

It is much more reasonable to assume that some idea of Schopenhauer's doctrines, which, as happens fairly often with works of genius, crystallised something already in the European air, came to Mallarmé from a fellow-poet, Leconte de Lisle.

The latter, again, had almost assuredly not read *The World as Will and Representation.* But thanks to his friend and master, Louis Ménard, and to the work of Eugène Burnouf, he was deeply impressed by ideas found in the philosophies of India (Schopenhauer had used the same source); and in the bulk of his poetry it is obvious that he accepts the view which takes all sense-data to be illusions, dreams engendered by the cosmic spirit when it objectifies itself. Hence his frequent allusions to the Veil of Maya which, cast over the empty abyss of Reality, makes us believe that we see an infinite number of minor realities, valid in themselves.

Indeed, if we were looking for a 'source' for *l'Après-Midi,* we might just as well seek it in Leconte de Lisle's poetry as anywhere else. We might quote, for example, the great Parnassian's *Pan,* in the *Poèmes Antiques,* which contains many of the details found in Mallarmé's poem.

There are many ideas in *l'Après-Midi d'un Faune* that make

one think of *The Birth of Tragedy* and of Nietzsche's insistence
(due to the influence of Schopenhauer) on music as the art that
conveys pure Reality to us – the unfragmented beauty of the
world, without the blemishes of materiality. But *The Birth of
Tragedy* was not yet written when Mallarmé began the *Monologue d'un Faune;* and it would be rash to suppose that Mallarmé
ever knew anything of this masterpiece at a later stage in his
career. It is true, on the other hand, that by 1885 he had come to
know and to accept, probably without knowing that it was
Nietzsche's, the argument put forward in *The Birth of Tragedy*
that, after the decline of tragedy in Greece, the only nation to
revive it (through music) was Germany. For in an article,
Richard Wagner. Rêverie d'un Poète français, published that
year in the *Revue Wagnérienne*, he writes 'Avec une piété
antérieure, un public pour la seconde fois depuis les temps,
hellénique d'abord, maintenant germain, considère le secret,
représenté, d'origines'.

What is really important, however, for our present purpose, is
the fact that *The Birth of Tragedy out of the Spirit of Music*
was written some six years after the *Monologue d'un Faune,*
and was thus in process of incubation while Mallarmé was still
working on the early drafts of his poem. So-called literary influences are often strongest and most significant when they are
indirect; when they are not so much influences as utilisations
of a common source.

In this way, two men who have never heard of each other
may well throw out, more or less simultaneously, ideas that are
singularly cognate. This well-attested but rather neglected fact
might well explain why the young Nietzsche and the young
Mallarmé (the French poet was about two years older than the
German thinker) both attributed enormous importance to music.
And both had an immense admiration (though it was not without reserves in Mallarmé's case) for Wagner.

Mallarmé's actual knowledge of Wagner's operas was indirect.
He had not witnessed any performance even when he wrote the
article quoted above. But he was a fervent admirer of Baudelaire's work, and Baudelaire had been one of the first in France
to extol the work of the German master.

In any case, it is certain that in *l'Après-Midi d'un Faune*
Mallarmé, like Schopenhauer and Nietzsche, looks on music as

an art that transcends the plastic arts; an art from which he always wished that poetry should 'reprendre son bien'.

What does 'reprendre son bien' really imply? For one thing, it entails an adaptation of musical technique to poetry: hence the interwoven and subtly recurrent themes of which *l'Après-Midi* consists and which have already been discussed in the present study.

'Reprendre son bien' also entails a radical transformation of the poetic image. Music, which transcends imagery and adumbrates the pure Idea behind images and phenomena, is often full of *suggestions* (one of Mallarmé's desiderata), which seem almost to engender images – though obviously they can never do so, for sound cannot become sight. As we listen to a musical masterpiece, say a Beethoven symphony or sonata, or one of Wagner's best overtures, we have the feeling that we are almost seeing images, or that we are about to see them. Baudelaire discusses this with eloquent lucidity in *Richard Wagner et Tannhäuser* (1861).

These suggested 'images' in music loom up, or seem to loom up, so that one almost *sees* a great sweeping upwards towards cosmic spaces; or has the feeling that a landscape is about to come into view; or half expects some cosmic sorrow to emerge as a visible figure, a Niobe recalled from the darkness of death and draped in death's immensity.

Naturally, these images never emerge from the ocean of sound in which they seem to be hidden. They almost reach the surface, but are engulfed again in that harmonious sea; rise once more, and once more, only to disappear afresh. And so the imagination waits in vain, in the same way as the Faun vainly waits to see the two nymphs emerge from the darkness of sleep in which he had lost them. The imagination waits in vain, but there is a strange pleasure, defying analysis, in the waiting; a nostalgic yearning that softens into the sweetness of recognition whenever a lost image almost returns – until at last the music ends, leaving a silence which is no longer empty, but full of echoes that are audible to the inner ear and images that are still unreal but which haunt the inner eye. Are the echoes images, or the images echoes? Actually, neither images nor echoes exist; they are part of our pure imagination, void of materiality.

In other words, 'Music is', as Schopenhauer said, 'when seen as an expression of the world, a general language in the highest degree, which has approximately the same relationship to the generality (Allgemeinheit) of concepts as the latter have to individual things. Its generality is, however, in no way the empty generality of abstractions, but of quite another kind, and is bound up with a clear and universal exactness. In this it is like geometrical figures and numbers, which (are) the general forms of all possible objects of experience' *(Geburt der Tragödie,* 16, where Nietzsche quotes this passage from *Die Welt als Wille und Vorstellung).*

Music has the same general but non-abstract, satisfying yet nostalgic beauty, in the definition given by Mallarmé in lines 44-51 of *l'Après-Midi.* Here the Faun realises that as he played his pipes, the visible beauty around him, 'la beauté d'alentour', was taken over into his song; and that the physical, material, visible beauty of feminine bodies was transformed into 'Une sonore, vaine et monotone ligne.' Music, as he sees it, is 'vaine', because it is empty of individual realities; 'monotone', because its near-images never materialise. Yet he remains, with conviction, a musician.

These near-images that never materialise, so characteristic of music, are to be found everywhere in Mallarmé's work, where their very elusiveness gives them an unforgettable beauty and provides an answer to those who complain that his poetry is unnecessarily difficult. But never, perhaps, did the poet pour them out so profusely as in this, the most musical of all his poems. They make the *Après-Midi d'un Faune* difficult to follow. But then, it is not necessary to 'follow' it in the conventional sense, except in so far as it is written with words, and words, as I have said earlier, necessarily tell some sort of 'story'. That is the only justification for the exegesis given earlier. It helps the reader (I hope) to feel more strongly the nostalgic beauty of 'musical' images for ever almost rising to the surface and constantly reabsorbed into the musicality of the whole.

How closely these elusive images in the poem resemble the inchoative and unmaterialised 'images' of music is actually demonstrated by the 'argument' discussed in our Interpretation. For although images of the nymphs loom up in many different forms, they never become concrete or really visible. And however carefully we examine the poem, we can never discover – nor could the Faun – whether the two nymphs really existed. They emerge as symbols of sensuality, as memories, as imaginings, as art-forms, as nostalgic dreams; but they can never be revealed. This is impressionism pushed to the point where nothing remains, and yet everything remains; just as, in listening to pure music, we can see no phenomena and are yet in contact with something that lies behind all phenomena.

This 'something' was for Nietzsche, at the time when he wrote *The Birth of Tragedy*, as for Schopenhauer also, the pure source of all phenomena. Such a virtual identification of music with the Absolute seems to me, however fascinating, dogmatic and unproven; but it was widespread in the 19th century.

.   .   .   .

We still have to ask why Mallarmé had his three memory-passages printed in italics. Obviously he wished them to stand out from the rest of the text. The most feasible reason that I can imagine for this is not an easy one to formulate; and I must ask the reader to bear with me if the exposition is somewhat lengthy.

The Birth of Tragedy, as we have seen, is posterior to the gestation of the *Monologue d'un Faune*, but is a manifestation of the same Zeitgeist, with differences that are inevitable owing to the gulf that exists between French and German cultural traditions. And in Nietzsche's essay we find an argument that may be most revealing with regard to the problem we are examining.

Nietzsche maintains that in Greek tragedy the plastic and verbal element is necessarily subordinated to the musical, but is yet indispensable. The two are complementary; without this combination, spectators would not have the lesson of tragedy brought home to them (we can leave aside Nietzsche's peculiar symbols, Apollo and Dionysos, which would here only confuse the issue). He finds this alliance between music and plastic art in the Wagnerian opera – of which *The Birth of Tragedy* is, as much as anything else, a defence. The scenes, the actions, the words are a kind of prop needed by the spectator or listener. They are a visible symbol of individuation; a symbol which makes the undifferentiated totality of the cosmos less remote, more acceptable.

To put it in a less metaphysical way, let us extract from the young Nietzsche's romantic overstatements their core of psychological truth and say this: The more exquisite and incantatory the pleasures of hearing become, the more they need to be completed by the pleasures of sight and explanation. Man wants to understand as well as to be exalted. He lives in a kingdom of light, and his soul cries out for visual beauty, plastic forms, lucid dialogue.

That is one reason why most of us like good ballet. The moving figures, the forms and colours that emerge out of the music, are not the images that we seem to foresee in the musical structure itself; but they are closely enough wedded to the music to give the eyes the festival that they have been awaiting. There is a haunting theme in the second act of Tchaikovsky's *Nutcracker Suite*, for example, that, to me, always suggests, in a dim, elusive, nostalgic fashion, a path leading upwards into regions of romance, with horns softly sounding for a moment as each new vista of imagination opens out. When this is interpreted by a corps de ballet moving forward and retreating in mass formation, as if aspiring to the unknown and hesitating because of its inaccessibility, what I *see* is not at all what I *heard;* but it introduces harmonies of a new kind, a suave series of accords between sight and sound, a sweet alliance between the two senses that play the paramount role in humanity's aesthetic experience.

It is interesting to find that Mallarmé himself seems to have noticed this transformation, in the ballet, of music into visible forms. In a passage of *Autre Etude de Danse: les Fonds dans le Ballet* (1893), he writes:

'Le décor gît, latent dans l'orchestre, trésor des imaginations; pour en sortir, par éclat, selon la vue que dispense la représentante çà et là de l'idée à la rampe. Or cette transition de sonorités aux tissus (y a-t-il, mieux, à une gaze ressemblant que la Musique) est, uniquement, le sortilège qu'opère la Loïe Fuller, par instinct, avec l'exagération, les retraits, de jupe ou d'aile, instituant un lieu.'

His prose is here, as usual, rather precious and cryptic; but it seems to me that his argument is as follows: Scenery is not essential in a ballet; it is already *inherent in the music* ('Le décor gît, latent dans l'orchestre'), which offers a wealth of suggestions to the imagination. This invisible spectacle emerges, in all its beauty, as soon as Loïe Fuller begins to dance. Her movements in themselves create an adequate scene ('lieu').

There is no escaping the intention of the phrase 'cette transition de sonorités aux tissus', which must surely allude to the transformation of music into filmy visibility.

The Faun offers himself a similar metamorphosis when he reconstructs his memory-pictures. They lift him out of the somnolent sensuality of his mood; satisfy the plastic artist who, along with a musician, dwells in his soul. The italicised passages are rather like the scenes and dialogues in an opera, the illuminated figures in a ballet. And for that reason, perhaps, Mallarmé makes them stand out by means of special typography. *His italics are like footlights* suddenly turned on in a darkened theatre, when the overture finishes and the curtain rises.

To keep up this analogy, we can add that as the poem ends, the curtain falls again, the footlights go out, and the last vestiges of plastic beauty pass away in the phrase : 'Je vais voir l'ombre.'

This explanation seems to be corroborated by the poet in the remarks made in the course of an interview for which Jules Huret had asked him on behalf of the *Echo de Paris*, in 1891. They are quoted by Henri Mondor in his *Vie de Mallarmé* (Paris, Gallimard, 17th edition, 1946, p. 600). I italicise the phrases which perhaps help to explain the italics in *l'Après-Midi*:

'Vers 1875, mon *Après-Midi d'un Faune*, à part quelques amis, comme Mendès, Dierx, Cladel, fit hurler le Parnasse tout entier, et le morceau fut refusé avec un grand ensemble. J'y essayais, en effet, de mettre à côté de l'alexandrin dans toute sa tenue, une sorte de jeu courant pianoté autour, comme qui dirait *un accompagnement* musical fait par le poète lui-même et *ne permettant au vers officiel de sortir que dans les grandes occasions.*'

Is it not possible that among these 'great occasions' are the moments when the plastic stands out against the musical background in the three beautiful passages which are, in the text, printed in italics?

. . . .

The Faun is disturbingly human : like man as Pascal saw him, he is *ni ange ni bête*, and yet is both. His sensuality is quite animal, but he is capable of exquisite notations and sublimations. The artist in him, painter and musician, lifts him out of his animality and sublimates his hot dreams into music and into pictures alternately.

He is to some extent Mallarmé himself. The latter had in him a strong fund of sensuality. Yet in it there was always a certain indifference, the dreamy aloofness of the artist. This frequently, in his poems, sublimates the pleasures of the senses into something like the Faun's 'sonore, vaine et monotone ligne'. One of the clearest examples is in *Mes bouquins refermés . . .* where he is sitting at the fireside with his mistress; but while their passion seems to stir the fire ('notre amour tisonne'), his thoughts are elsewhere. He is less delighted by the warm reflections on her breast than by what they suggest: the burnt breast of an amazon, lost in the inaccessible depths of mythology, and yet not lost. Once more an absence has proved more seductive than a presence; art's idealism has risen above the flesh:

> Je pense plus longtemps peut-être éperdûment
> A l'autre, au sein brûlé d'une antique amazone.

This is another way of saying that, for poets carried on the current of nineteenth century idealism, the phenomenal world is never quite real. A beautiful form, a beautiful body, is not wholly satisfying in itself. It is only a Representation (in the sense in which Schopenhauer uses 'Vorstellung') of pure beauty, which is absolute and undividuated. No woman, however fair, can embody ideal perfection for Mallarmé. A nymph may satisfy the Faun's animality; but because he is an artist, she can never be wholly real. She is only a symbol, and he seeks in vain for the Reality behind the symbol. Even music can only adumbrate this supreme Reality, leaving it incomplete and somewhat empty, in 'Une sonore, vaine et monotone ligne'.

Music, as conceived by Mallarmé (and his Faun), brings us nearest to the inaccessible Reality. But in this respect his idealism goes even further than that of Schopenhauer and Nietzsche: music does not quite bridge the gap between the ideal and ourselves. A marginal territory remains, a fringe of incompleteness due to the imperfections of man and his instruments.

Matter cannot identify itself completely with spirit; and musical instruments are made of matter, they create vibrations in a material atmosphere. Hence Mallarmé's cult of *silent music,* still in the composer's mind; the 'souriant fracas originel' *(Hommage à Wagner)* still unwritten; 'les vols qui n'ont pas fui.'

Perhaps it is this feeling of his own inadequacy and that of his instrument that makes the Faun speak as he does to his syrinx in lines 52-53:

> Tâche donc, instrument des fuites, ô maligne
> Syrinx, de refleurir aux lacs où tu m'attends.

Those poor reed pipes are only two pieces of dead matter, after all. And for that reason they are, in two senses, an 'instrument des fuites'. They not only startle the nymphs into precipitate flight, but also, by their imperfection, drive off Reality just as it is almost attained. The Faun is here speaking from the level of his frustrated sensuality; but perhaps the artist in him is speaking from a level nearer to the stars.

V

Critical Epilogue

In studies of poetry I have always thought it best to speak
from inside the text; to adopt, for purposes of interpretation,
the poet's point of view. But having done that, I wish in the
present instance to judge the *Après-Midi* from the outside, in
relation to Mallarmé's work in general.

Much as I admire his work, I cannot honestly refrain from
saying that there is at times a certain artificiality in it. His
poetic method is so subtle, and he has devoted so much time
and attention to it, that occasionally method becomes for him
an end in itself. I am not here objecting, of course, to his putting
a veil over his images and letting the light shine through it
from within; not only do I not object, but I even think that this
method gives the *Après-Midi d'un Faune* a haunting, inimitable
beauty, and creates precisely the sort of atmosphere required:
the atmosphere of a drowsy interlude between one dream and
another. But in some of Mallarmé's sonnets the veil, though its
texture may be intrinsically beautiful, allows nothing intelligible
to show through.

That is because he occasionally forgets that method is not an
end in itself; that the veil must not be a mere texture of words.
When he thus falls into the trap of his own subtleties, he leaves
himself open to the reproach of inventing word-puzzles. In such
cases he does himself a double disservice. He gives adverse
critics a stick with which to beat him; and he leads too many
of his admirers into the temptation of thinking that elucidation
is their sole task, whereas it should be only a beginning.

This deliberate obscurity is perhaps a recrudescence of sub-
jective idealism; not the big, creative, almost objective idealism
that inspired some great figures in both French and German
romanticism, but one that tempts the poet to arrogate the right
of creating his own private world.

A private world is an edifice of *états d'âme*. Mood has its lawful place in poetry, undoubtedly; but the poet's business is to communicate his mood adequately. Mallarmé quite justifiably maintained that in poetry suggestion is a better instrument of communication than statement. But communication still has to be adequate, and pure hermeticism is to be ruled out, unless the poet is composing only for himself. And though Mallarmé stressed the value of silent music, and talked of 'vols qui n'ont pas fui', he obviously envisaged an audience: otherwise he could have come closer to his ideal of perfection by not writing at all.

I have set out these criticisms frankly, not to take away from the reader's appreciation of the *Faun,* but rather to enhance it. For on the background of these defects in certain sonnets and, I am afraid, in the *Cantique de saint Jean,* the *Après-Midi* stands out as a poetic masterpiece. It is, in fact, one of the most exquisite and really poetic poems ever written.

It is rather thickly veiled in places; but the consciousness that Mallarmé is communicating is drowsy, uncertain, nebulous, and this calls not for clear images, but for the *suggestion* of imagery that characterises music. Never elsewhere did the poet more convincingly and more exquisitely demonstrate that the miracle is possible; that poetry actually can take back from music at least part of what belongs to it.

Whether Mallarmé here took back only a part of what he considered to be the property of poetry, whether he here made poetry do all that music can do, or whether this latter miracle is conceivable: these are questions to which I have not yet discovered an answer. Perhaps that answer is hidden in the text of this and other poems; and I hope to devote some time to the search for it.

For the moment, I can only say that if *l'Après-Midi d'un Faune* is completely musicalised, Mallarmé must have discovered some way, as yet not discerned by those who have studied the poem, of adapting to poetry the rules of harmony. In music, the component parts of a chord are heard simultaneously; but as two words cannot be pronounced simultaneously (unless there are two speakers or readers), harmony in a poem would have to take the form of vocalic and other echoes; the chords would have to run, as it were, *along* the lines, or down through the architecture of the stanzas. This may, perhaps, be less difficult that one would at first suppose; for I imagine that in poetry chords could be built with ideas as well as with sonorities. One idea can vibrate in unison with another, as is actually the case in many of Mallarmé's best poems.

But even if he has solved this problem, another remains. Listening to music, what the ordinary music-lover hears is, above all, the melody of the treble clef (that is how we all recognise a tune). But a trained ear can discern simultaneously *the melody of the bass*. Was Mallarmé aware of this, and did he find a way of maintaining this second melody in his verse? So far, I have discovered practically no evidence of this. Yet I am tempted to think that the problem had not escaped his notice.

In the difficult and often misinterpreted sonnet that begins with the lines

> A la nue accablante tu
> Basse de basalte et de laves

'tu' refers to the sound of 'une trompe' in line 4; most appropriately, for the sonority of 'tu' (and of 'nue') is acute. And *under* the line where 'nue' and 'tu' occur, we find, not only in the deep sonority of the four a-vowels, but in the meaning of the words, what might well be called a bass melody.

This example is not fortuitous, for so careful and subtle a poet as Mallarmé does not owe his effects to accident; but on the other hand, it may be unique.

In any case, the musicalisation of the imagery in *l'Après-Midi* is so successful as to be almost miraculous. And even one miracle in this difficult domain is sufficient to vindicate the poet's claim (in the preface to *Un Coup de Dés*) that it is possible to borrow back from music 'plusieurs moyens m'ayant semblé appartenir aux Lettres'.